Here and There

Teakie Welty

Illustrated by Kenny Estrella

Copyright © 2013 by Teakie Welty. 138833-WELT

ISBN:	Softcover	978-1-4931-0320-1
	Hardcover	978-1-4931-0321-8
	EBook	978-1-4931-0322-5

All rights reserved. No part of this book may be reproduced or transmitted in any form or by any means, electronic or mechanical, including photocopying, recording, or by any information storage and retrieval system, without permission in writing from the copyright owner.

Rev. date: 09/26/2013

To order additional copies of this book, contact:
Xlibris LLC
1-888-795-4274
www.Xlibris.com
Orders@Xlibris.com

*in memory of my high school sweetheart
and husband of 54 years*

Alan McKean Welty Jr.

When I am home,

and I am HERE,

I often wonder

what's happening THERE!

Is Grams jogging,

or is she sitting?

Is she cleaning,

or is she knitting?

Is Grampa out

by the woodpile chopping?

Or did Grams send him

to do the shopping?

Is Mom at work

or is she flying?

Is she at the store,

and what's she buying?

Is Dad in the office,

running the show?

Or is he fixing the car –

making it go?

Is my sitter at school

studying hard?

Or is he at home,

cleaning the yard?

Is the park filled with kids

having fun?

Is someone swinging

on my favorite one?

Is my school all quiet

and oh, so neat?

Or could someone else

be in my seat?

Is my TV lonely

without me there,

laughing at the shows

from my favorite chair?

Are Sarah and Alan

hard at play?

Is Mikayla being good

or bad today?

Are Maddy and Morgan

playing in the rain?

Is Charlotte taking

a ride on the train?

Are flowers blowing

in the breeze,

scattering pollen

which makes us sneeze?

If the sun is out,

where is the moon?

Are the stars still twinkling,

even at noon?

When you are at home,

and you are HERE,

do you often wonder –

what's happening THERE?

Edwards Brothers Malloy
Oxnard, CA USA
October 16, 2013